BATTLE MiLK 2

Tangents and Transitions in Concept Art

Published by

designstudiopress.com

Designed by

transitcreative

transitcreative.com

Battle Milk Volume 2: Tangents and Transitions in Concept Art

Copy Editor: Christina Apeles
Book Design: Michael Long/Transit Creative

Published by Design Studio Press
8577 Higuera Street
Culver City, CA 90232
Website: www.designstudiopress.com
E-mail: info@designstudiopress.com

Printed in Korea.
First edition, July 2010

10 9 8 7 6 5 4 3 2 1

ISBN: 978-1-933492-53-7

Library of Congress Control Number: 2010926742

CONTENTS

Foreword	6
Introduction	7
Wayne Lo	8
David Le Merrer	28
Thang Le	48
Kilian Plunkett	68
Le Tang	86
Jackson Sze	106
Artist Bios	126

FOREWORD

For generations before I was born, telling a story in a visual medium relied solely on an artist's drawn or painted renderings. With the advent of motion pictures, artists had an entirely new set of tools to work with. Some used those to transport audiences to fantastic, faraway places that previously existed only in their imaginations. I never dreamed that someday I would contribute to that creative process in a way that would reach millions of people. As a matter of fact, it was a fortunate series of coincidences that led to my working as a concept artist on the original *Star Wars*.

In the years since I retired, I have had the opportunity to review a great deal of work by young, upcoming talent, such as the artists represented in this volume. It always pleases me to see art with a distinct, signature style. While the tools artists use today may be more sophisticated than the pencils and brushes I relied on, the fundamentals remain the same. Clarity. Simplicity. Form and shape.

There was a period in my life when I felt that I should spend more time focusing on creating fine art, as opposed to the design work that I had produced through much of my career. While I do have personal pieces that I remain fond of, I discovered there are also examples of my design work that I appreciate just as much. Designers quickly learn that while it may only take a single image to "sell" a concept, the effort required to arrive at that is the challenge that they face on a daily basis.

Every artist approaches the blank page inspired or influenced by the artists they admire, as well as their personal experiences. The six illustrators in this volume have taken what they have learned while working on *Star Wars: The Clone Wars* and drawn upon their imaginations to create new, original works of art. I believe this is one of the most important things anyone interested in design can do. I hope you enjoy their explorations as much as I have.

R. McQUARRIE

Ralph McQuarrie
Berkeley, CA
April 2010

London, ©2010 Ralph McQuarrie.

INTRODUCTION

Why *Battle Milk*? The name was a tangent; a misinterpretation of a less ridiculous suggestion. As little sense as it made then, it makes perfect sense now. The title reflects our varied personalities and has now come to represent our very artistic diversity.

Battle Milk Volume 1 showcased the unique stylings of Kilian Plunkett, Thang Le, Wayne Lo, and Jackson Sze. This time around, fellow Lucasfilm Animation colleagues David Le Merrer and Le Tang were brought into the fold, bringing even more variety to the mix.

Battle Milk is a vehicle for us to stretch our creative muscles beyond the 9 to 6 workday. All the things we want to do as individuals take center stage, rather than conforming to an overall unified style. These pages are filled with work we are compelled to create, the things we are moved to utter.

We hope you enjoy what we have to say.

9/27/8

WAYNE LO

Beneath the Canopy

Originally, my sketches explored images of plump, cheerful fairies jumping into the arms of good-natured, robust sprites. My drawings later steered toward a clandestine love affair between a wild faun and naive dryad. Speckled by a rosy afternoon sun, the pair embrace in the cool shade. In contrast to the dryad's amorous enthrallment, I was hoping that the faun's presence would communicate a smoldering, sinister undertone, giving it another layer of drama.

Forest King

Memories from my favorite high-school wilderness inspired this piece. Here, stone, tree and fox spirits bend to pay homage to the forest king. Three unruly sprites cower beneath the penetrating gaze of the arboreal prince. I imagine this could be a comforting thematic counterpoint to that of the faun and dryad image (opposite), especially for protective fathers of dryads.

She Spies a Pool Party

The watercolor piece (right) appeared originally in the catalog for a charity auction whose proceeds went to help protect an inspirational forest just outside urban Tokyo, through the ecological agency founded by legendary anime director Hayao Miyazaki. The theme of the project challenged artists to draw upon their own childhood interactions with nature as inspiration for their pieces (or at least that's how I remember the theme). This treasure trove of inspiration resulted in a pile of illustration ideas from which I chose this small story. I have included an earlier sketch (above) to show how differently and similarly my early inklings and final piece turned out. I think I finished the pencil sketch not long before our first daughter was born. In fact, the image was inspired by my own musings, imagining her as a toddler playing in our backyard. Now that she's born, I find a surprising resemblance between her and the little girl in the picture! But then, her brother looks similar too. Oh well.

Robot Myths and Legends

Several years ago, a group of friends and I decided to tackle a short story about a little robot and her adventures in a large, mechanized world. This spread showcases a range of sketches inspired by Art Deco appliances and architecture, as well as toddlers, elementary school-age kids, and a variety of other sources.

I got around to giving names to a few of them. Below, with the wing nuts on her head, Kimi skates by on her hoverblades. On the far right of this page, Lil' sports an oversized backpack and robo-visors perched above her forehead.

Mimi-Z

One of my favorite bot characters and sketches, this petite robot sprouted from a variety of inspirational sources. In particular, I tried to abstract and recombine orchids (specifically lady slipper orchids, I think), 1920s fashion, and a pair of white shoes, as well as the general Art Deco style range we'd targeted. Topped off with a bright neckerchief, Mimi-Z came to life for me as a bright, reserved, and surprisingly resilient little robot girl.

Black Turtleneck Variants

Here are four attempts at desecrating a classic.

In the form-fitting version in the third image (from left to right) on the facing page, the turtleneck almost becomes the centerpiece of the outfit. With a gifted figure, the black silhouette from all angles becomes an elegant, enticing graphic, with enough simplicity to complement rather than compete with a beautiful face. The flat silver chords swirl around the torso in sweeps, flashes and sparkles. To provide another level of interest, the sleeves from shoulder to wrist are sheer and detailed with a subtle inlaid pattern.

The two sketches that bookend this spread (far left and far right) represent the most extreme, youthful tweaking on the black-turtleneck theme. It combines a tube top, choker, and sheer bodysuit with tattoo-like swirly patterns from the wrist up.

In the second sketch on the opposite page, the turtleneck performs more of its classic role, using simplicity to frame the wearer's face and cloak-like outer garment.

Another take (right) made from thicker, slightly ribbed material fits at the further end of the age spectrum from the tube top/bodysuit version. I imagine an enhanced hour-glass figure achieved through structural pinching and loosening of materials.

Warrior Rats Protagonist Pen and Ink Sketches

This block-headed newbie finds himself initiated into the ranks of a vicious race of rodents. Smiling naively in the top right sketch, before long he knows better than to look beyond his blinders, snarling on cue and at the slightest slight of slights (low central image).

Warrior Rats Anatomy Sketch

As part of an anatomy exploration exercise, I painted up one of my pen and ink line sketches. Here I haven't really addressed weapon and gear design. In the end, this pass feels a little bit too human to me, but not a bad start.

Warrior Rats Color Sketch (below)

Lean, mean killing machines with long teeth and surly attitudes, this race of rats is not to be trifled with. This character group shot explores various body types, faces and personalities (as well as weapons and gear) in relation to each other.

Eyes on the Prize (right)

Whipped into a desperate, ruthless frenzy, our youthful initiate growls through pulled-back cheeks with a grimace fit to greet all comers. The taste of blood electrifies the air as the dust rises and the sun blazes. His father would be proud.

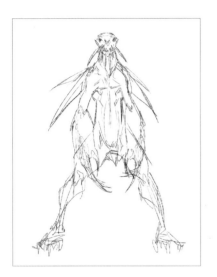   

Step 1: Black and White Sketch

I chose this design from a pile of brainstorm and exploration sketches for a swamp-dwelling or an otherwise aquatic creature. Even with all the diverse sources of zoological inspiration swimming in my mind, I made it my goal to imbue the design with some of the essence of a giant catfish. this particular sketch turned out to be a particularly humanoid take on the catfish abstraction theme.

Having already taken a more straight-forward approach to rendering the creature under imagined studio lighting and stage conditions for another illustration (see the next two spreads), I wanted to let things develop a little more randomly this time. Free of other production and logistical constraints, I just wanted to have some fun with the piece.

Step 2: Randomizer

I started by laying down some random shapes of varying hue, value and texture. After turning the canvas several times obliquely, mirrored, upside down, and right side up, I began to get a rough idea of what I was seeing in my "mess."

I then added some marks to start to define a figure, its basic gesture, and a faint suggestion of a background. For quick reference, I placed a separate multiply layer of the chosen design sketch in the top right corner.

Note: The "straight-ahead" approach taken to create this illustration is just one of many possible approaches that I use in tackling assignments. More often than not, a series of compositional thumbnails and sketches come first, before I go into a final. Digital media lends itself well to this "straight-ahead" approach, which can be quite a fun and freeing change of pace.

Step 3: Blocking and Gesture

In this step, I've begun to lay down the structural foundations for the main figure in my piece, sticking to faint suggestions of light and shadow under ambient lighting conditions for now.

By now, I think I'd begun to get a clearer picture of what I wanted this creature to develop into. Rather than keep him in a swamp environment, for the sake of a more dynamic image, I decided to place him among the crashing waves of a rocky coastal setting. He becomes less of a catfish creature and maybe more of a catfish/salmon/sea lion creature.

Step 4: Lighting

Here I started to sculpt the figure with light. A warm bounce light reflects off the rocks below. A bluish sky provides a general fill light from above. To pick out the structure of the creatures head and shoulders, I imagined a slightly diffused sun providing a sort of backlit situation.

Step 5: Final Touches

To finish up the image, I further defined anatomical and environmental details (e.g., crashing waves, sea spray, claws, and musculature). To provide more dynamic lighting contrast, I cranked the effects of the backlit sunlight, imagining the sun poking out through thinning clouds and reflecting off the creature's wet, scaly hide.

I added the assault rifle, blood spatters, and hand to the image almost as an afterthought, to turn the illustration into more of a storytelling "portrait." If these elements seem a bit tacked on compositionally, it's probably because they are. I'm not totally satisfied, but I am happy with them as a dynamic second-or-third-read "reveal," telling us just a little more about our critter friend.

Step 1: Swamp Creature Sketch

I approached this image as a creature design illustration, appropriate for use as pitch or design material for feature films and visual effects. The main goal would be to exhibit the creature with clarity in a fairly photographic style, with imagined studio lighting and stage setting. I wasn't too concerned about overall composition, thinking that the background would be incidental, primarily there to give the design some context.

I picked a sketch from the same pile of exploration doodles (same pile from which the sketch for "Crash" came, in the previous spread). This was applied as a multiply layer over a muted background, suggesting a "swampy" night scene. I hinted at forms by blocking in a key light from above, to the right, and slightly from behind."

Step 2: Photo Scrap for Skin Texture

My next step was to gather some photo scrap to collage together some skin texture for the creature. Since my core concept was to create a swamp creature inspired by a giant catfish, I gathered an array of high-resolution digital imagery of catfish (and other large aquatic animals).

I cut and pasted, transformed, and color-shifted the material, being careful to fit forms and not create too much hue contrast.

What you see here is all that reference, refitted, and flattened as a normal layer.

Step 3: Initial Lighting Pass

I then turned the photo scrap/collage layer into an overlay layer. All the subtle hue and value variations become more apparent as an overlay. This will have to be toned down for the final image, but it also provides a rich, varied color base.

Of course, the photographic texture and detail start to show through as well. Again, this doesn't fit the forms and anatomy precisely, but that will be addressed through paint.

My first step painting is to pick out sort of backlit sheen along the back, shoulders, and head of the creature (to help emphasize the slickness of wetness of his scaly hide).

Step 4: Key and Fill Lights

To more clearly separate the values of the forms hit by the imaginary key light from those of the region in shadow, I used the levels adjustment tool to brighten the key lit areas.

Then I turned to sculpting the subtly lit regions, with an imaginary, ambient-like fill light. To pull the creature away from the background, I hinted at a warm low-angle backlight coming from screen left.

Step 5: Back Light and Paintwork

Here I continued more of the same work. The backlit edges were brightened a little. More detail in the ambient/fill zone was painted in.

The paint work here was done using various settings from the brush generator and some of the standard textures. Particular brushes are less a concern than fundamentals, though suggestive matching of the existing textures is still important.

Step 6: Background and Final Light

To create a foundation for the background, I pulled together digital imagery of forests, jungles, streams, rocks and swamps. I loosely followed some of the rhythms found in my initial lay-in. My primary concern is to create a stage for the main figure and to not compete with it for attention. Getting the rhythms to flow will help make a dynamic and pleasing overall feel for the image.

I've known that I wanted the swamp to be a misty environment, and here I've started to hint at some of the mist in the foreground and far background.

The final stage (over) was to paint over the background photography (so everything lives in the same world stylistically), play up my rim lights, refine my other light sources, and extend the background to match parameters requiring a landscape format.

DAVID LE MERRER

ELLIOTT'S SUPERNATURAL TALES

From childhood's hour I have not been
As others were; I have not seen
As others saw; I could not bring
My passions from a common spring.

— *Edgar Allan Poe*

Elliott is a project I started while still at school in Paris. It is an idea for an animated TV series that features a main story arc, a main quest as well as side stories.

These are the first images I did back then. My main inspiration was Tim Burton's work and Edgar Allan Poe's poems. The excerpt on the left page, from Poe's "Alone" poem, inspired me to define Elliott's personality.

These two images illustrate examples of screen titles, inspired by 1950s and 60s TV series. In European folklore and mythology, ravens are known as the ghosts of murdered people, souls of the damned...

Who is this mysterious crow?

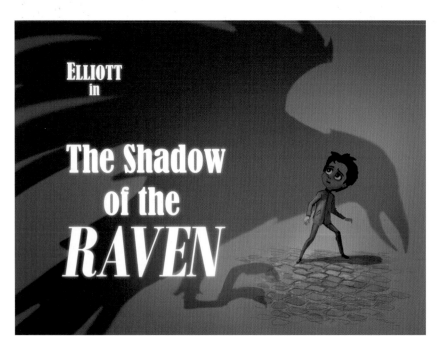

De la terre à la lune
Içi le temps a tout estompé
La lune éclaire de ma lanterne
Ce cimetière triste et terne
Devenu une terre de paix
Là git sous trois pieds la rancœur
Et à ses côtés la bêtise
Juste derrière les fausses crises:

Les trois maux de touts mes malheurs
Les mains de l'arbre montrent le chemin
Simple de la terre à la lune
Voyage éclair au clair de l'une
De marbre où se joignent nos mains
Au delà des grilles: les collines
Où j'irai trouver les mots tendres
Attendus à qui sait attendre
Calme et serein: sa divine

— Yves Le Merrer

Elliott discovers these Celtic megalith stones. Later on, he will learn that the giant monuments are portals to other dimensions.

The concepts done for this book illustrate what would be the first episode of the series. Elliott escapes his uncle's manor, several nights before his escape he has nightmares showing him things he doesn't really understand, the only thing he knows is that he belongs to something else and something fantastic is waiting for him. At the end of the episode, he will encounter this mysterious crow that will change his life forever.

These illustrations show Elliott wandering around thinking about his destiny. I don't know if this sequence will eventually happen during the fall or winter.

The milkman discovers Elliott unconscious, lying on the road early in the morning. He will take care of him.

After Elliott escapes his home, the policemen investigate his disappearance. The small one is inspired by the amazing actor Louis De Funès in the French movie *Le Gendarme de Saint-Tropez*. He doesn't look like him, but like him in his temperament: grumpy, impatient and very choleric.

The manor of Elliott's uncle.

Elliott's favorite spot in the nearby city.

Preparatory sketches for the full-spread painting.

Step 1: Thumbnail

First I do a quick sketch for the composition and leave the middle part of the image without any details or important elements as it is a full spread.

Step 2: Color sketch

Then I did a color study without going into detail, just trying to capture the lighting and atmosphere with few brush strokes.

Step 3: Line Drawing

If I am happy with the composition and the color study, I start to draw the different elements of the image and the perspective better. I usually draw the characters on another layer.

Step 4: Details and Refinement

When I am finished with the line drawing, I start to paint the final image, following the small color thumbnail I did earlier. Most of the time I still design the image while I paint.

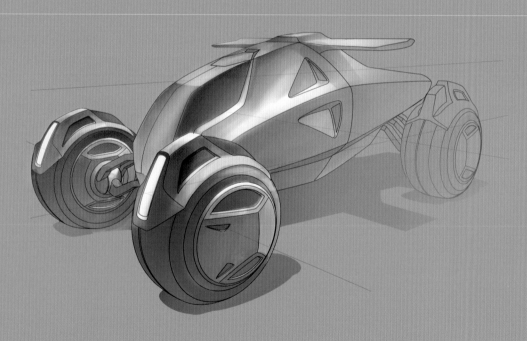

THANG LE

Man has always sought to go beyond his own limits, to discover and to explore. Space is no different. Arthur C. Clarke argued that it is humanity's choice to essentially expand off the Earth into space or face cultural and biological stagnation and death. The human race simply cannot sustain itself given the lack of natural resources, the population growth, as well as epidemics, disasters, and war. It is with this thought that man sought expansion into space. To go beyond the terrestrial boundaries and expand his reach. It is man's nature to discover, explore, and expand. To adopt foreign territories and make them his own. To find new resources to cultivate. To go beyond, where he was never meant to be.

Daedalus Base, Far Side of the Moon

Built by ISO (Inter Space Organization), the Daedalus Base is located on the floor basin of Daedalus Crater, also known as Crater 308. The base is the site of the solar system's largest communication telescope and launch facility. The base itself is constructed mostly beneath the moon's surface to shield it away from solar winds and radiation. Its location and geography is ideal to minimize interference caused by Earth's communication emissions. The facility is constructed mostly out of lunarcrete, building material formed from lunar regolith.

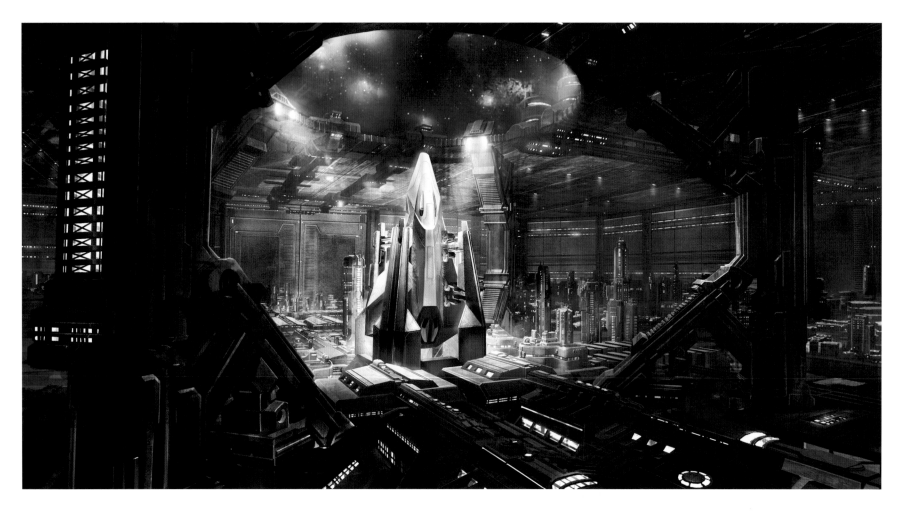

Daedalus Launch Facility, Far Side of the Moon

One of eight launch pads within the Daedalus Base. The launch site for the new Titan Shuttle. The Titan Shuttle is ISO's latest innovation in deep space exploration. Powered by Helium-3 nuclear fusion, the Titan Shuttle is capable of going beyond Mars to the reaches of the solar system's gas giants. It is designed with the ability to enter and exit out of the gas giants' atmosphere. It is ISO's intent to explore and mine the vast Helium-3 mines in the atmosphere of Jupiter, Saturn, Uranus, and Neptune.

The Daedalus is in proximity to an abundant source of Helium-3 found on the far side of the moon. The moon's regolith is mined and the isotope is extracted all within the surrounding area. This precious isotope is used in fusion reactors that power most of Earth's terrestrial and extra terrestrials operations.

Daedalus Launch Facility, Far Side of the Moon (above)

The Launch facility lies below the surface of the moon. The high terraced walls of the crater shield it from the sun's solar winds and harmful radiation. The low gravity on the moon is ideal for shuttle launches into space.

Daedalus Launch Facility, Far Side of the Moon (left)

The Titan Transport Shuttle is the newly developed transport vehicle designed by ISO. It was created and built for exploration of the surrounding gas giants. Its exterior is built from space-age bio composites, similar to Earth-based plants that absorb the sun's ray for nutrients, the shuttle's outer skin is capable of regeneration and repair.

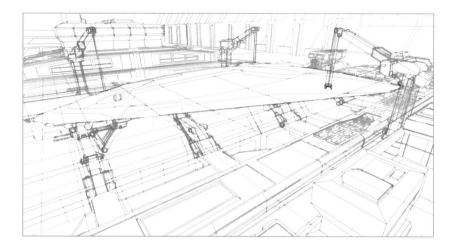

Step 1: Line Drawing

First, rough out the composition of the image. Then establish perspective lines to help build the space of the environment. Start by blocking out the design with simple shapes. Next, refine the design and begin drawing in simple detail.

Step 2 : Blocking in Shapes

Start by filling in the entire image with a mid tone. Then block out the individual shapes of the image. I begin to see if the silhouettes of the design work. Next is to start defining the objects with a directional light source.

Step 3: Refinement

The majority of the image is blocked in at this point. Edges are starting to be defined and designs are further worked out. I begin to edit the image and design accordingly. I work out the design of the shuttle separately and once it is finalized it is reincorporated into the image. Between the refinement stage and final image, I decided to add an additional trussing system above the shuttle to redirect the eye towards the shuttle. It also shows depth by overlapping elements.

Titan Shipyard, Far Side of the Moon

Kronos Deep Space Carrier (above)

ISO developed a deep space vessel with the intention to travel beyond Earth's solar system into the deep reaches of space. It has six arms that function as solar sails and energy collectors. When closed, the arms protect the majority of the main structure from radiation and destructive rays. When opened, or fanned out, the Kronos has three runways. This allows for the departure and landing of different spacecraft.

Within the Kronos, there is a completely developed, man made ecological system. Kronos's ecosystem consists of different biomes, all created to resemble the biosphere of Earth. It is ISO's hope to not only sustain the crew and future generations of the vessel's inhabitants, but to also plant the seed for future Earth, like colonies beyond our solar system.

Kronos Deep Space Carrier (opposite)

The carrier has three runways to accommodate departures and landings. The center ring is the vessels main control center. Kronos' bridge, communication, and control towers are all located within the center rings. The outer structure of the Kronos is the carrier's hanger bay and storage facilities. Amongst Kronos' fleet of space craft is ISO's Titan shuttle. It will serve as the ship's reconnaissance vehicle during its deep space venture.

Aias Power Suit

The Aias Power Suit was designed to allow its pilot to easily work within the harsh environment of space and extra-terrestrial settings. It was made primarily as a construction vessel, though the suit can be outfitted for other needs including combat and exploration.

The Aias overcomes the human deficiencies normally attributed to space. It is equipped with systems capable of long durations in extra terrestrial environments, systems that include life support, communications, mobility, and environmental protection. The suit also gives its pilot extra human strength and agility. ISO created the suit to be easily constructed and maintained. The four limbs are identical in design and are interchangeable when necessary. The main body opens from the front to reveal the cockpit. The suit exterior is made from composites with an underlying metal alloy skeleton.

Aias Power Suit, Kronos Deep Space Carrier

Icarus Rover

The Icarus is a one man rover designed for short-range exploration. First used for reconnaissance on the surface of the moon, it has been refitted for use on Mars and other similar terrain. Its open wheel design and off road agility allow it to navigate through the most difficult environments. The main body houses the cockpit and life support systems, while the four wheels house the Helium-3 fusion motors and gravitational devices. The weight of the vehicle is distributed equally atop the four wheels. Its exterior is built of solar deflecting composites that keep the driver safe from harmful radiation.

Helium-3 Harvester (above)

The Harvesters are built to withstand the harshest extra terrestrial conditions. They are capable of working in the extreme warm and cold temperatures of space. They have been used on the surface of Earth's moon and neighboring planets Mars and Venus. The Harvesters have been not only used to extract Helium-3, but also repurposed for scientific studies. The machines are able be retrofitted for deep core drilling and geological ground sampling.

Helium-3 Harvester (opposite)

ISO's harvester is a massive machine created to mine, process, and store Helium-3 isotope. It is supported by six identical legs that are attached to the main ring. The drill column is lined with blades that tear through the densest ground material. Within the blades are filters that, when in motion, cut through and process the Helium-3 isotope from the surrounding matter. The central column absorbs and stores the nuclear matter within its central chamber. When the chamber reaches capacity, the drill column is removed and replaced. The column itself then becomes a storage chamber for the Helium-3 isotope, similar to a nuclear fuel rod.

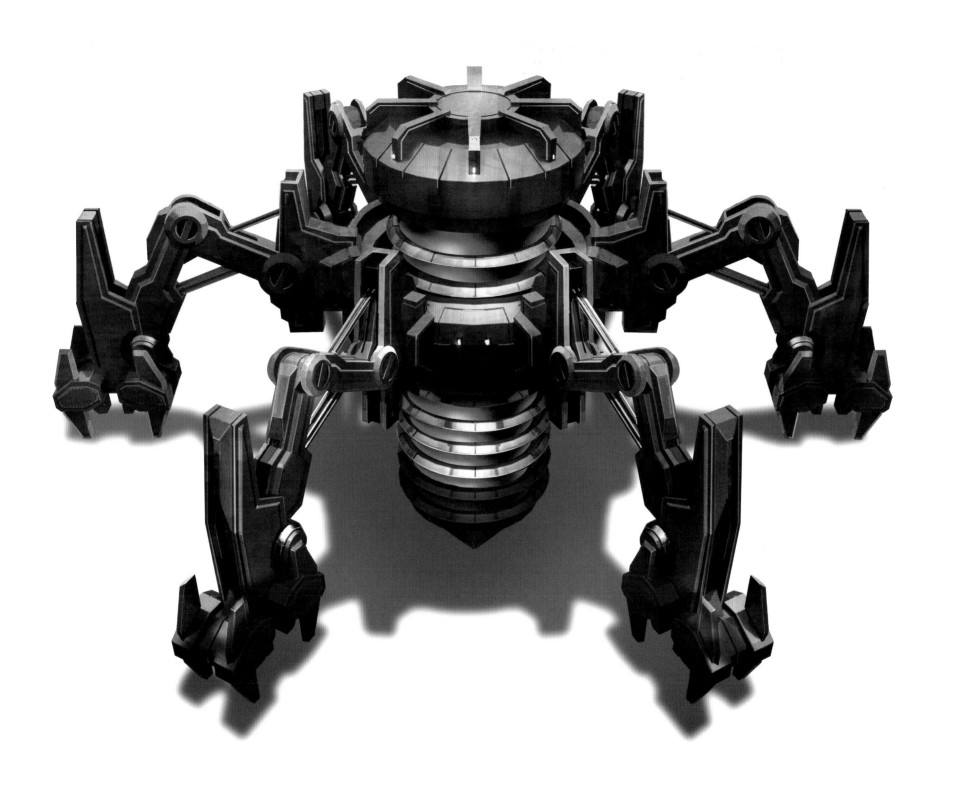

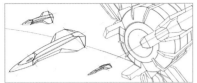

Step 1: Thumbnails

The intent of this piece was to create a dynamic action shot. The design of all the elements used was figured out before starting. I started by thumbnail sketching out different compositions, figuring out what would best show dynamic movement, scale, and be interesting to the viewer. I ended up choosing the last thumbnail. I liked that the shuttle was coming toward the camera and leading the viewer's eye towards the secondary subject, the carrier, and the size relationship between the two vehicles.

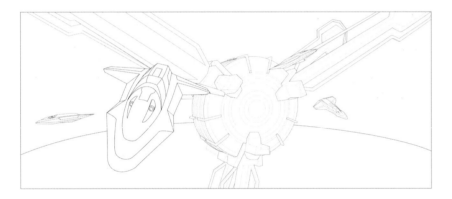

Step 2: Line Drawing

Once the general composition was chosen, I began to define the objects with a more accurate line drawing. I can do this by simply creating an overlay layer in the computer and drawing right on top of it. I kept in mind perspective, proportion, and shape. I drew in the majority of the large and medium shapes, leaving smaller details and cut lines to be added later in the painting.

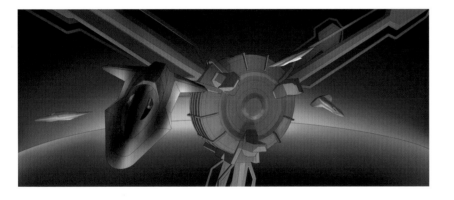

Step 3: Blocking in the Elements

I knew that the painting was going to be set in space where the major light source would be from the planet below. The first step is to fill the entire painting with a mid tone. This allows me to judge value easier than working on a white background. I then mask all the separate elements and begin generally defining the different planes of the object. I continually flip-flop the image, to check balance and composition, making adjustments when necessary.

Step 4: Defining a Light Source

As stated earlier, I knew the major light source was going to be from the planet below. I then started working on all the elements keeping that in mind. All the surfaces facing the planet would be lighter in value and so would the objects' color. I also thought about contrast, because objects with higher contrast draw the eye first, while objects with lower contrast tend to become secondary. At this point, I introduced warm and cool color elements. Typically, warm colors come forward and cool objects recede, though I wanted to show that the planet light source is warmer than the object's local color.

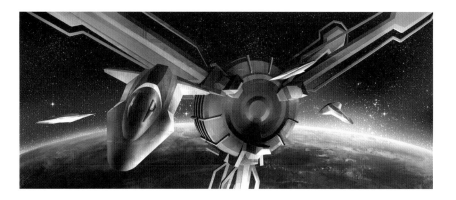

Step 5: Refining the Shapes

The majority of the painting is already defined: the general lighting, color, and feel. At this point I begin to resolve complex surfaces, define edges, and design medium and smaller elements. I push and pull objects to create depth and atmosphere. I add secondary light sources to define the vehicle's different planes.

Step 6: Details

All the large and medium elements of the painting are done. I start thinking about small shapes and greeblies, accent lights and colored markings, to show the scale of the objects. Cut lines are added to the surface of the foreground shuttle to help reinforce the shape. I then begin painting highlights in certain areas to draw in the eye of the viewer. At this point, the painting completed.

KILIAN PLUNKETT

A final composition can come about in many ways. Several initial loose sketches of submersible leisure craft, in a similar vein to the *aerokraft* seen in *Battle Milk Volume 1*, led to this image. Though fun to draw, following the same retro aesthetic of the earlier designs, placing the subs in various tropical locales, wasn't achieving the desired affect. The "billboard" in this image in this image is part of the original direction I was going in while the rest shows where I ended up.

Why would mass-produced underwater rigs become widespread? If the worst predictions of global warming were to come true, many urban areas throughout the world could find themselves flooded. In the major cities, new forms of mass transportation would be called for. Boats might make more sense, but a personal submarine sounds like more fun.

MotoVolo

BOMBA
STANDARD CONTROL AEROPED

KMF-RATED (900 FT MAX ALTITUDE)

MEZZOCIELO™- CLASS AEROCRAFT BY THE MOTOVOLO COMPANY OF MILAN, 1962

The Bomba model Aeroped was first introduced in 1962 by the famed Motovolo company of Milan. The technology behind these flying machines is a closely-guarded secret, although it's understood to be electromagnetic in nature. The wings are too small to generate lift but their control surfaces are essential to the craft's manueverability.

The works of Hergé (Georges Rémi) were a big influence on me growing up. *The Adventures of Tintin*, set mainly in Europe of the 1950s and '60s, featured many vehicles of the period and their shapes and lines inform much in these designs.

This is a design that was "found" through kitbashing, a time-honored technique used in many film productions to help create miniatures. Kitbashing consists of combining different parts from a variety of plastic scale models to create something new. In this case, the main fuselage came from a water pistol while other parts are from a P-38 Lightning airplane and Ford hot-rod pickup kit.

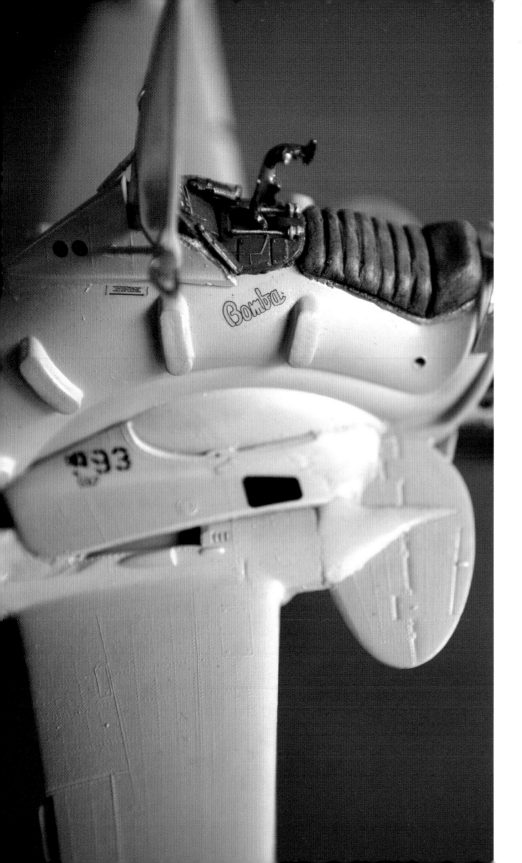

The windshield and seat were the last pieces to be added since the overall scale was undecided until the landing gear was in place. The name "Bomba" came from cutting a decal from the P-38 kit that read "Bombardier" in half. A lot of the appeal of kitbashing is its improvisational nature.

Orbital space stations have been the subject of many images in print and on film. Since the stark imagery of Earth from space is so visually arresting, it makes for a compelling canvas to work against. Following the thread of vehicle designs derived from existing forms seen in nature, the framework for this space platform is based on dragonflies.

Whenever a vehicle or structure is designed for use in an extreme environment it comes with a sense of drama and tension built into it since any major failure will result in catastrophe. The absence of gravity opens up possibilities for shapes and configurations that might be hard to justify on terrestrial mechanical designs.

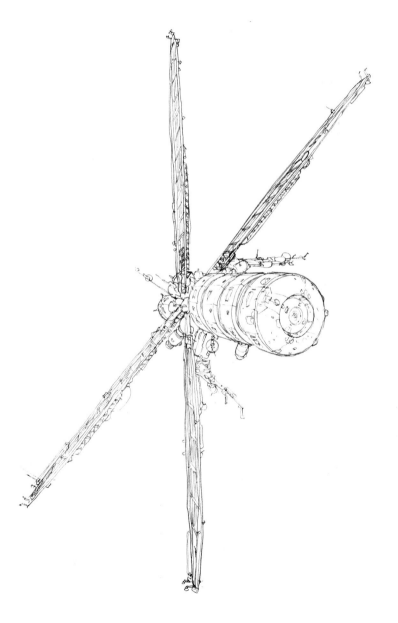

Another staple of science-fiction illustration and design is the mechanical exo-suit. A concept that's been around since the 1950s, it has appeared in many media, perhaps most successfully in the works of Kow Yokoyama. There are endless permutations to explore, which explains the enduring appeal of the basic idea.

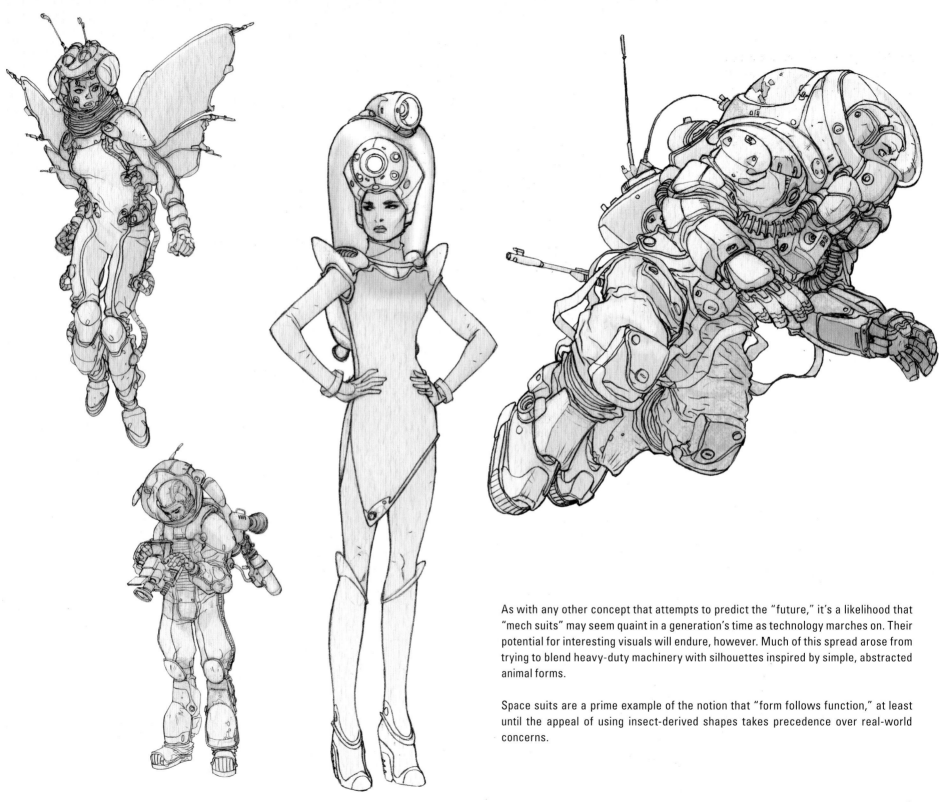

As with any other concept that attempts to predict the "future," it's a likelihood that "mech suits" may seem quaint in a generation's time as technology marches on. Their potential for interesting visuals will endure, however. Much of this spread arose from trying to blend heavy-duty machinery with silhouettes inspired by simple, abstracted animal forms.

Space suits are a prime example of the notion that "form follows function," at least until the appeal of using insect-derived shapes takes precedence over real-world concerns.

The initial approach I took to the space platform section of this book was more along the lines of the cartoon-like feeling of the "Bomba" pages. As I started adding surface details, they informed the aesthetic more than the basic shapes, and I reworked the characters to fit into the more "realistic" feeling environment. One of the most satisfying aspects of working on a design is the way the image itself will eventually lead you in a specific direction, even if it's an unexpected one.

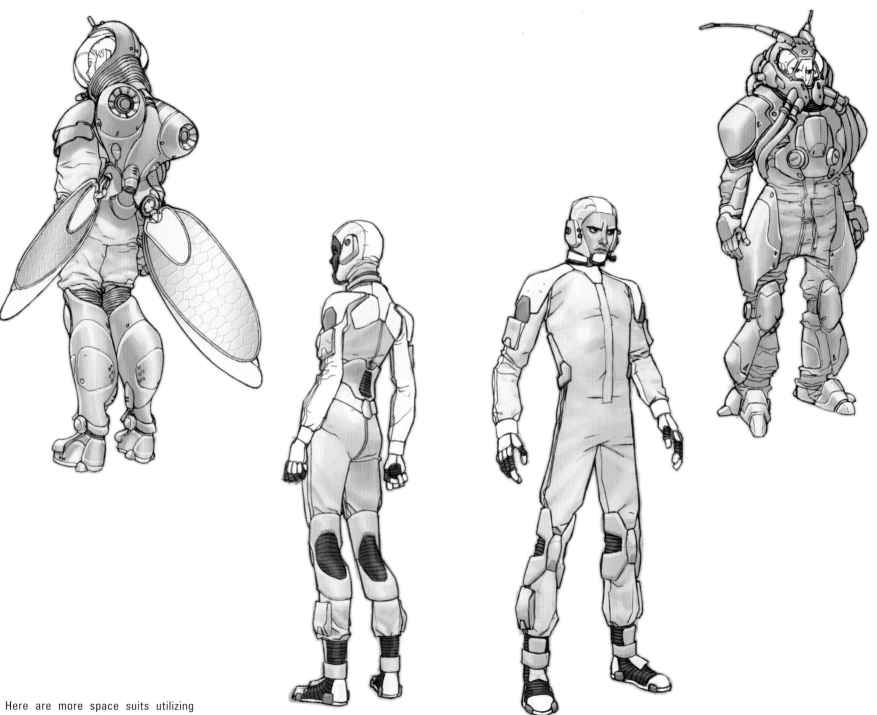

Here are more space suits utilizing animal forms as jumping-off points.

Step 1: The Premise

The goal of any entertainment design is to help tell a story. Epic tableaus and heroic characters are often the focus of the design process. I'm of the opinion that the small moments can matter as much as spectacle. Usually, life onboard a Space Station seems filled with either perfect, high-tech efficiency or dramatic, dire peril. Chances are high that human error and technical failure would be inevitable. A few quick marker sketches roughed out the main idea in order to find where the emphasis would lie; in this case, the hapless traffic controller.

Step 2: Preliminary Sketch

Designs from *Battle Milk Volume 1* depicted a more typical sci-fi "space kitten" outfit in which exposed skin trumps practicality. In this case, I wanted to stick more closely to a realistic, functional suit, but still relate it in some way to the earlier version.

A tighter pencil drawing of the main character was worked up. The details on the suit and headgear were kept loose enough to allow for adjustments.

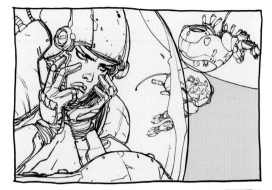

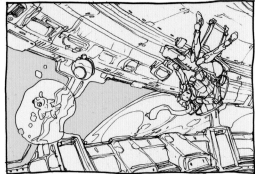

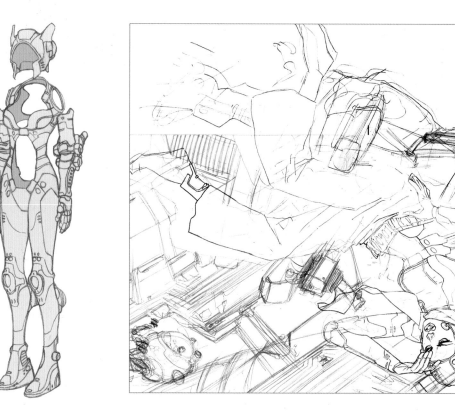

Step 3: Composition

Knowing the dimensions of the "canvas," the various elements are moved around until a satisfying composition was found. At this stage, the overall layout was decided.

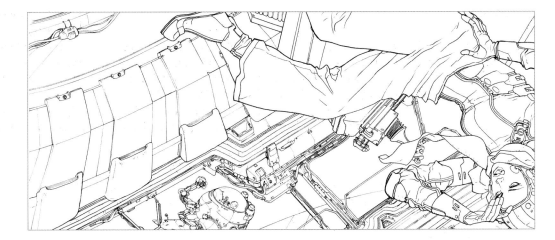

Step 4: Palette and Values

The palette and lighting were intended to reference classic Hollywood spacecraft interiors of the 1970s. Knowing that the star field outside the window would be a stark near black affected the surrounding values and contrast.

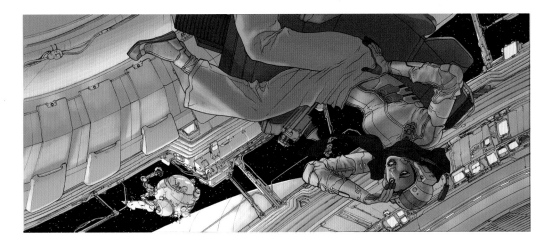

Step 5: Final Touches

To help sell the feeling of extreme cold, the image takes on a largely blue cast, and any warmth is kept in the foreground. Some experimentation with using Photoshop's ability to blur sections of the image results in a 'racking focus'.

Overleaf: "Business as usual"

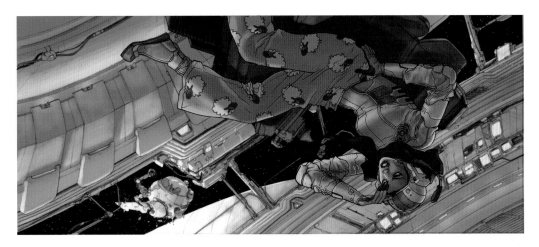

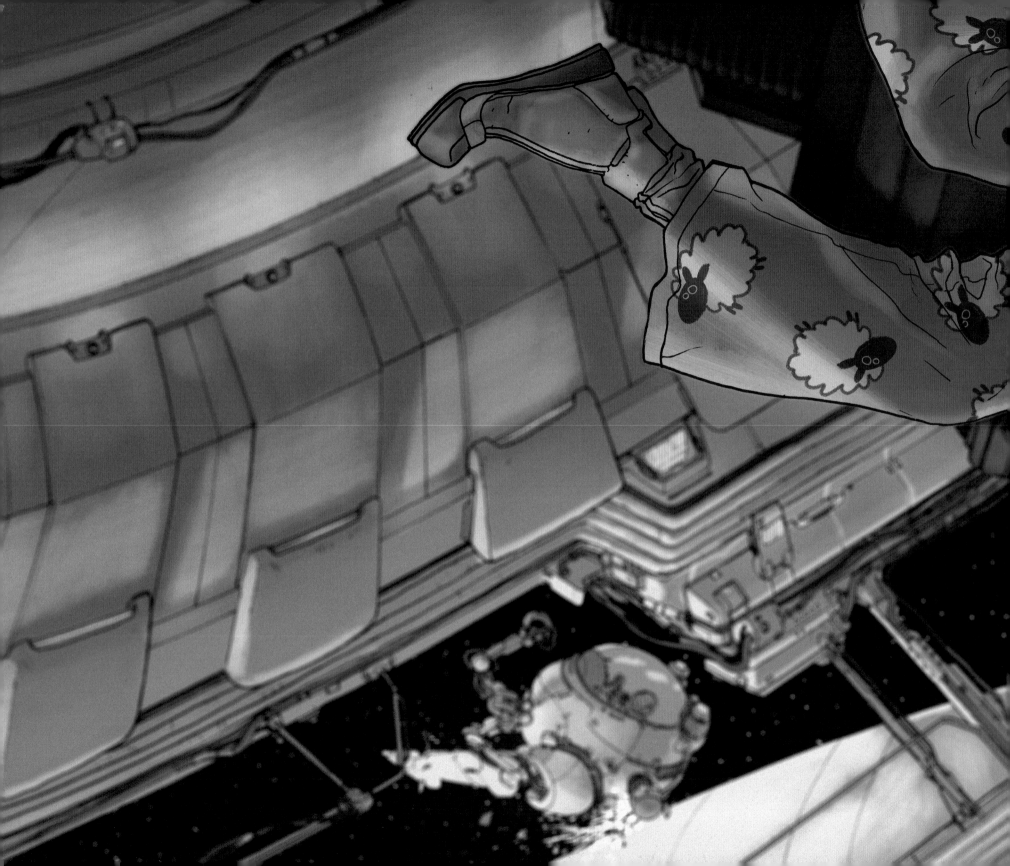

LE TANG

The idea for this piece actually changed a bit from the original scribble. Earlier on, the image depicted a long line of children waiting for their turn on the rocket-ship ride. As I delved deeper into the idea of a child's imagination, the line of children seemed to emphasize more the rocket itself than the idea of where a child can take it. So I decided to eliminate the line, but it now threw off the balance of the image. Fortunately, placing a trusty ol' dog came to mind. Even though it was an afterthought, I feel the dog brings a lot of charm to the image.

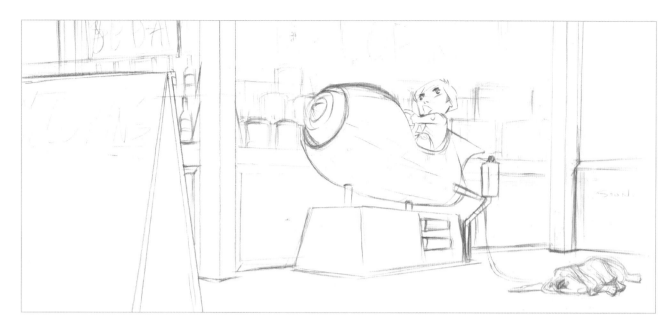

These are some character studies I did of Gabriel. I used very simple, soft, round lines in the early stages of his design to create playful shapes. I had to minimize the size of his head in proportion to his body. Even though it added a lot of character to him, it made some poses difficult to achieve.

Mom (OS and from afar): You better be awake... *Mom:... You'd rather I not...* *Mom:... have to come up there!*

Mom: Trust me!

 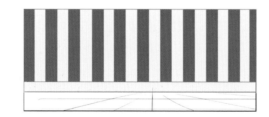 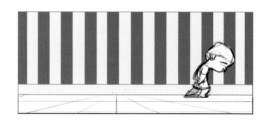

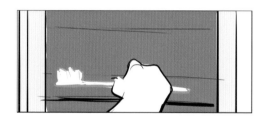  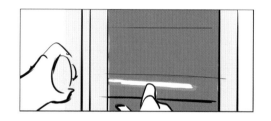

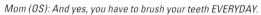

Mom (OS): And yes, you have to brush your teeth EVERYDAY.

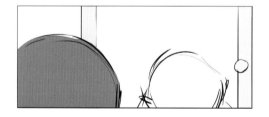  

I grew up in the midst of a martial arts craze. Images of heroic underdogs defeating the villains with lightning speed and powerful fists were not foreign to me. So I placed Gabe in a very familiar daydream.

It's no coincidence that children are often the centerpieces of my work. Much of my work comes from a child's perspective: looking at the world with curiosity and wonder, having more questions than presumed answers. Children don't understand the impossible; they haven't been "educated" in it yet. Limitations are still foreign to them, ultimately promoting their creativity and innovation.

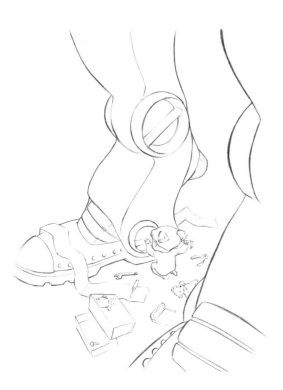

In both these pieces, I played with contrasting scale, having the children small in comparison to their creations. I intentionally hid the faces of the children to make them more relatable.

Hot Shot Du Jour: friend to all, lover to many.

A man of mystery, a man of adventure, a man of seduction. Men bow to his confidence, while women faint at his gaze. He carries with him at all times a cigarette, his lucky lighter, and an unflappable aura of sophistication. He is the greatest thing to come out of France since sliced French bread.

I intended for this image of Hot Shot Du Jour to reflect not so much Europe itself, but a romanticized impression of it. I bathed the image in warm colors, offset with shades of purples to add to the sense romance. I contrasted his color and gesture with that of the girls to emphasize his calm demeanor.

The character of Hot Shot Du Jour originated primarily as a ridiculous name that eventually conjured up an image of a French pilot in my head. While designing Hot Shot, I steered away from making him physically appealing: heroic, strong-jawed, or muscle-bound. He's lanky and sports a large nose, making his charisma all the more impressive.

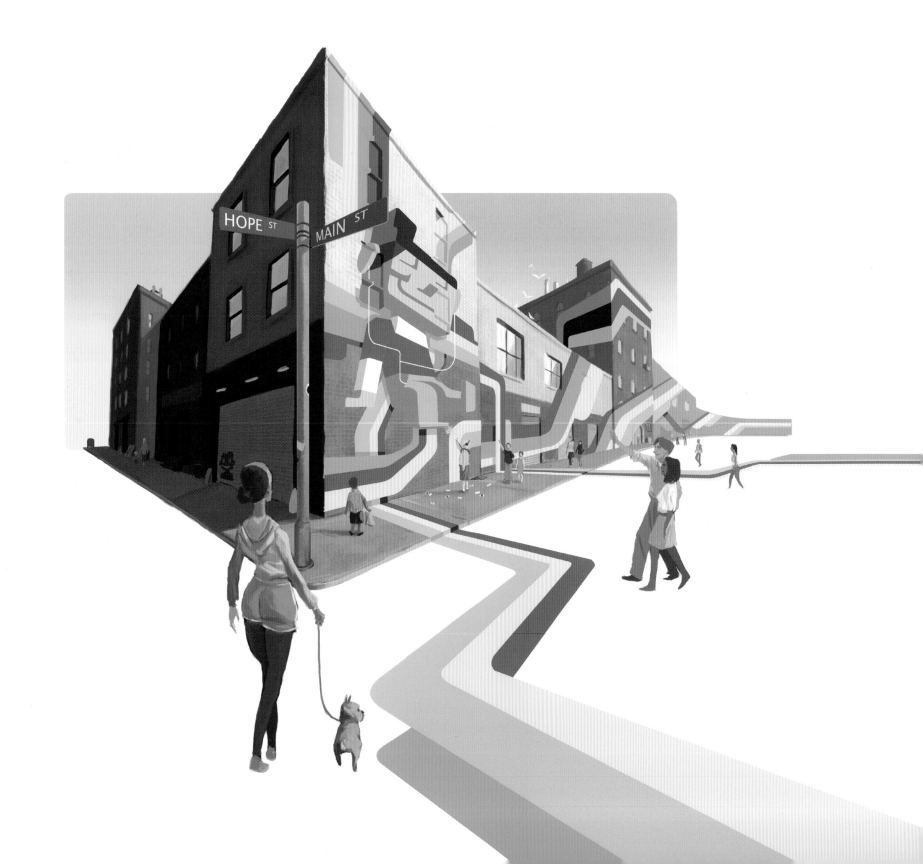

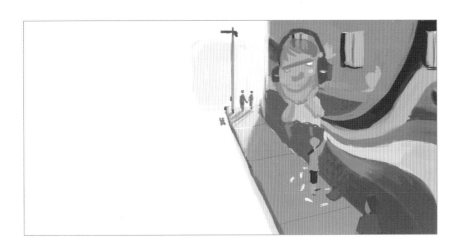

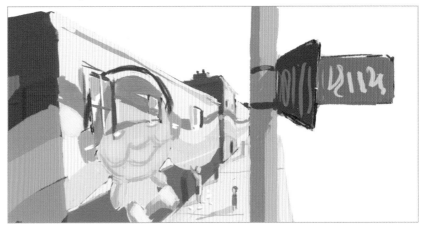

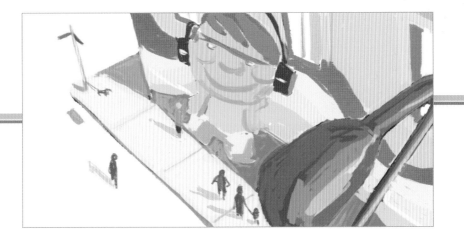

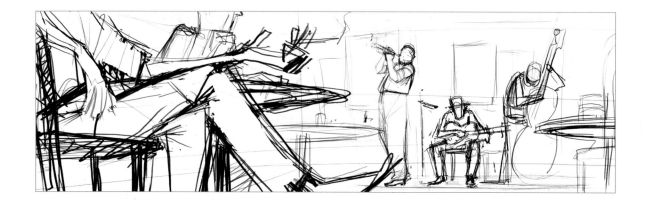

Step 1: Idea Sketch

I started with a small digital idea sketch. I just wanted to get a quick sense of the shapes, perspective, and composition of the piece. I positioned the audience and furniture on the sides of the image in order to frame the band, and made the foreground objects significantly larger than the band to add physical depth. I even cropped off the faces of the two men in the audience to really put the focus on the men on stage.

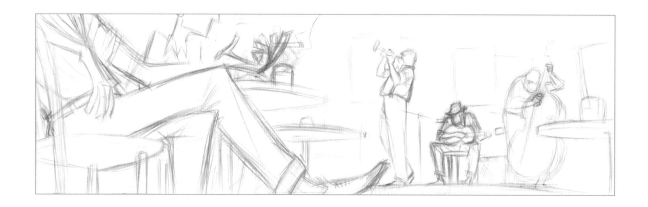

Step 2: Pencil Sketch

I transferred the idea sketch onto a sheet of 19-field animation paper, because I often times prefer the tactile sensation of sketching on paper with pencil. From there I made some fixes to problems that were not as prevalent in the smaller digital version, such as adjusting the angle of view of the stage. I also began to do more defining of the characters and instruments.

Step 3: Blocking in Colors

I wanted a very urban and nostalgic mood to the piece, so I centered the color palette to browns and other warm hues. Here I started to fill in broad bodies of color to bring out the abstract shapes and also sculpt out details in the band (faces, clothes, and instruments) that were not so pronounced before.

Step 4: Refining Background Elements

Since I worked in layers I was able to paint from the background to the foreground easily. I continued to work out the band with more detail, all the while understanding that they would have to be lit more prominently than anything else. I anticipated that the rest of the image would be dark, so I really tried to focus on bringing the most light and details to the focal point.

Step 5: Differentiating Foreground from Background

Here I continued to differentiate the background, midground, and foreground elements. By darkening up the foreground objects I added color depth to the physical depth of the piece, ultimately bringing even more focus on the band. Furthermore, I painted the foreground in broader, less detailed brush strokes to make it seem out of focus.

Step 6: Addressing the Entire Image

After adding the graphics and text to the posters, I began to address the image as a whole. I wanted a painterly texture to the piece and once all the different layers were in place, I began painting out the "seams". I did a paint pass on text on the posters so they would not be so crisp and further dimmed the areas that were not in the spotlight.

A poetry of sounds cut through the smoke, pitter-pattering and blaring from wall to wall. Brass and wood and string are instruments to men, but men are instruments to Music; a Music that releases itself from burning bellies and finds its way to the insides of friends, strangers, and everything in between.

A civilization on top of the world.

Perched on the highest mountain range, this is a place of mysticism,
grandeur, and adventure. What follows are snapshots of a culture
inspired by Tibet, reimagined and exaggerated.

Welcome to the Sky Kingdom...

Journey Begins (above)

The trek begins at the break of dawn.

By air, it will take travelers at least a day to reach the Sky Kingdom. From the border town of BakFong, hundreds of airships and hot air balloons lift off toward the sky. Travelers must follow the Dragon River towards the Northern Mountains.

The piece above is my humble homage to the great Kazuo Oga. His masterful background art can be seen in most Studio Ghibli films. Known as "the man who painted Totoro's Forest," his work and Hayao Miyazaki's films are the reasons I am an artist.

With reverence to their great legacy, we start on our journey...

Phoenix Point (opposite)

The formidable Northern Mountains guard the entrance to the Sky Kingdom. Here lie the highest mountain ranges in the world. The air is thin and temperatures are freezing.

Phoenix Point acts as a landmark for anxious travelers. Soaring toward the heavens, this part of the journey never fails to impress first-time fliers.

Rising thermals help lift airships pass the mountain peaks. Safety in numbers, the string of airships acts as a guide for each traveler.

Sky Kingdom Towns

These pencil drawings explore how buildings and whole cities can be laid out on a mountain peak. Pencil sketches force me to be more deliberate with shapes. It is also quite a meditative experience shading the sides of mountains. Rendering as I go, I carve into the mountains with the side of a pencil and just let the drawing grow.

Watercolor, pencil, 3D software, digital painting—the variety of mediums we can use to arrive at solutions is a great privilege when creating art.

Teton Pass (opposite)

Teton Pass is the official gate to the Sky Kingdom. Taking decades and thousands of workers to build, visitors are welcome to take a break from their journey here. Early settlements used to house construction workers evolved into entire towns and villages at the foothills of the gate.

I blocked out the giant buildings with simple 3D geometry, roughly textured the scene, and lit it as well. A painting pass afterward helped bring everything together.

Supply Shops (opposite)

There is another way into the Sky Kingdom. This involves a long journey on foot through hundreds of miles of mountainous terrain.

Large caravans and heavy livestock must travel this well-worn road. Here at the foot of the mountain, tea and supply shops help travelers prepare for the long road ahead. Some people just don't like flying.

Waterfall Crossing (above)

Paradise Climb is the name of the road into the Sky Kingdom. Steep slopes, waterfalls channeled from the melting snow, and thick forests are just some of the obstacles a traveler will encounter.

Here an intrepid merchant crosses a fast flowing river underneath the falls.

Temple

For this piece I started with massing in big shapes to define the composition. Once the picture was established, I rendered out the forms and added details for scale and a little bit of story.

I originally had the sun in the picture, but found it to be too dominating, so it was eliminated to keep the sky simple.

People of the Sun

This civilization, like many others, is dominated by its environment. Unique to the people of this place is the altitude of their cities. Being so high up in the sky naturally makes references to the heavens, a common practice in their culture. The other important entity in their lives will be the sun.

The locations are flooded with blue skies and buildings perched precariously over steep cliffs and mountains. I've tried to add some magic and culture, hopefully enriching this made-up civilization on top of the world.

The Sun Gate

This is a town square on the mountaintops. The giant gate is dedicated to the Sun God.

Tibetan buildings and decorations consist of vibrant colors set against sparkly white surfaces. I've tried to play up the color and fantasy here.

The main structure of the town square evolved from a round temple to a giant gate for more shape contrast.

Marketplace

The economy is the most important aspect of the Sky Kingdom. Why else would anyone travel all this way up the mountains?

It's fun to think of the different goods and services that are traded here, almost like an RPG town. You have your basic armor and weapon shops, textiles, precious metals, food, unique pottery, and crafts.

The painting on the right page is an exercise in ambiguity and suggestion. Hopefully I've not over-rendered the crowds and shops. The sights and smells of a wet market are best painted loosely, letting the viewer fill in the blanks.

I am drawing from my experiences in Hong Kong to add an ounce of authenticity to a scene like this.

Morning Mass (opposite)

It is time for mass when the giant bell rings, echoing throughout the mountains. The holy place for prayer is carved into the mountainside.

This piece started out as a marker comp. To keep things fresh, I really enjoy starting pieces in different ways and arriving at different shots and solutions.

A project in actual production will require almost every prop to be called out and illustrated. Here I'm exploring certain props from the hall.

Leaving (above)

Photography is used heavily in concept work. Though it speeds up production in some sense, making sure your work is still designed and not dictated by found photography require time and effort as well. The trick is to not make the painting look like a photo collage.

With his caravan full of exotic goods and pockets full of gold, our hardworking merchant is finally leaving the Sky Kingdom, traveling down the high cliffs, pass ancient ruins and worn trails.

What fantastical place is he going to next?

Step 1: Thumbnails

Knowing that this image will encompass an entire spread and tutorial, I explored some options before settling on a final image. The idea is to create an establishing shot for the kingdom.

Keeping in mind that the image will span two pages, I try to keep the center part of the image clear of important elements so as not to have them lost in the page gutter down the middle of the spread.

Step 2: Color Pass

Once the layout is selected, it's time to try out some color variations. There are a lot of predominantly blue images in this section already, so the warmer, more violet version at the right was chosen for contrast to the other paintings.

Step 3. Major Shapes

I begin with a violet wash over my black-and-white thumbnail and start defining the mountains in the background. Working from back to front, I paint pretty much the same way as I would approach a traditional watercolor landscape painting.

I definitely think about how the colors should work: strong, warm light on surfaces facing the sun, blue-violet fill light from the sky dome hitting top planes, and stronger contrasts as we come forward in the painting.

Step 4: Rendering

Here I continue to define the mountain shapes. It is a constant back-and-forth process adjusting how one shape looks against another. This goes for spacing, silhouette design, heights, and widths as well.

I am trying to get a variety of shapes and sizes to create what is hopefully a pleasing arrangement and balance.

Cloud layers are added in between mountain ranges to emphasize scale and depth.

Step 5. Details

Referring to my earlier exploration drawings and photo reference, I begin to block in the buildings. The big ideas of the image are established at this point.

Detail passes follow, then I continue to fine-tune shapes and proportions. I'm also designing snow patterns and shadow shapes. Lastly, airships are added to give the place a sense of life.

Jackson Sze

Wayne Lo

I was born on the East Coast, raised in California, saved in Cupertino, nurtured in Berkeley, rewired in Beijing, rebooted in Taiwan, shrunken-headed at San Jose State, discombobulated on Kerner Blvd. and jury-rigged into a VFX concept artist. There I cursed pirates, skinned werewolves, skewered vampires, thawed Neverland and got cluster-f*@ked on Iwo Jima. After about six years with the Industrial Light and Magic art department, I moved on to art direct Factor 5's PS3 title Lair. Since then I have been creating artwork for Lucasfilm's *Star Wars: The Clone Wars*.

www.wayneloart.com
www.waynelo7.blogspot.com

David Le Merrer

I was born in Paris where I grew up and later studied graphic design at ESAG met de Penninghen. After getting my degree I spent a few years in the UK creating art for video games. But after a while I grew tired of the rain and in 2005 the road took me to Northern California where I ended up in another video game company. Now I am working at Lucasfilm on the *Star Wars: Clone Wars* animated television show where I met all these crazy folks and decided to join the *Battle Milk* team.

www.david-le-merrer.blogspot.com

Thang Le

I was born and raised in Southern California. The youngest boy of seven children, I spent my childhood reading comics, watching movies, and playing video games. After high school, I moved to Pasadena where I attended the Art Center College of Design, majoring in transportation design. Prior to graduating, I decided to switch my focus to entertainment design. After receiving my degree, I began working in commercials, video games, and film. This eventually led to an opportunity to relocate and work on the *Star Wars: The Clone Wars* animated television show and film. After several years at Lucasfilm, I decided to move back to Southern California to pursue other creative endeavors.

www.thangle.com

Kilian Plunkett

It's hard for me to believe that, growing up in Dublin, Ireland, I would one day end up gainfully employed drawing and painting the kind of robots, monsters, spaceships, heroes and villains that occupied so many of my waking hours as a pale young geek. I moved to the US in the early 'nineties when the chance to work as a professional comic artist came along. Comics taught me the value of learning to draw as broad a range of subjects and settings as I could. I worked almost exclusively as a comic artist until 2005, when an opportunity arose to be part of the team at Lucasfilm's new Animation division. I've been there ever since, learning everything all over again.

www.kilianplunkett.blogspot.com

Le Tang

I have spent most of my years in Southern California, but woke up from a stupor one day to find myself living in the Bay Area. I studied animation and studio arts in Southern California, but on the job is where the real education started. My career so far has been short-lived, ranging from being an animator on small traditional animation projects to a story artist on the 3-D television show *Star Wars: The Clone Wars*. Be it short, it has still been sweet. Now I'm gonna cross my fingers, knock on wood, and hope this good fortune keeps up.

www.letang79.blogspot.com

Jackson Sze

I've always liked to draw and paint. My passion grew as I was exposed to video games, cartoons, and movies. Creating worlds is infinitely exciting. Thankfully my parents were always supportive of my passions. I studied illustration at Art Center College of Design with an emphasis in entertainment arts. Since leaving school, I have worked in advertising, video games, television, and film. With luck, I was brought into Lucasfilm Animation where I eventually worked on *Star Wars: The Clone Wars*. Now I'm back in Los Angeles, teaching and freelancing for games and films.

www.jacksonsze.com
www.jacksonsze.blogspot.com

ARTIST BIOS

SPECIAL THANKS

Many people have assisted, guided, mentored and, in general, helped us to become the artists we are today. We can't thank them all here, but there are a few people who specifically helped us out with this book: Michael Long, Scott Robertson and Tinti Dey.

Wayne Lo would like to thank his family and God, the Lord Jesus Christ for His sacrifice, boundless love, endless grace and, well, everything...

David Le Merrer would like to thank Han Park, Ralph McQuarrie, and Stan Stice. Ralph doing our forward is amazing! Thank you so much! And Michael Long for his great book layout and help. Thanks Mike! David would also like to thank his family for always supporting him in his passion, with a special thanks to his wife Johanna for her love and for always being there for him through his French grumpiness.

Thang Le would like to thank his parents for their encouragement, his siblings for support, and especially all his little nephews and nieces who inspire him with their limitless imagination.

Kilian Plunkett would like to thank Han Park, Stan Stice, Ralph McQuarrie, Michael Long of Transit Creative for the book design, Joel Aaron for his photography, his family and Catherine for her endless, inexplicable tolerance.

Le Tang would like to thank the support of his loved ones, the education of his failures, and the humility that comes from with working with such talent. And also the inventors of delicious cheese products.

Jackson Sze would like to thank his family, Iain McCaig, Erik Tiemens, Kevin Chen, and Bill Perkins for their time and generosity. And special thanks to Scott Robertson and Tinti Dey of Design Studio Press for helping to make this project a reality.